D1216159

The purpose of this study guide is to provide supplemental educational material. It is not intended as a substitute or replacement of THE HATE U GIVE.

Published by SuperSummary, www.supersummary.com

ISBN – 9798673644652

For more information or to learn about our complete library of study guides, please visit http://www.supersummary.com

Please submit any comments, corrections, or questions to: http://www.supersummary.com/support/

TABLE OF CONTENTS

OVERVIEW

The Hate U Give is a young adult novel published in 2017 by the American author Angie Thomas. The book's protagonist is a 16-year-old Black girl who witnesses a White police officer kill her friend. A *New York Times* bestseller, *The Hate U Give* won several awards, including the American Library Association's William C. Morris Award for best debut and the Coretta Scott King Award for the best children's novel by an African American author. The book appeared on the National Book Awards longlist for young adult literature, and it received a nomination for the Carnegie Medal in 2018. Due to its profanity and themes surrounding police brutality, *The Hate U Give* was also one of the top ten most-challenged books of 2017 and 2018, according to the American Library Association. In 2018, director George T. Tillman adapted the novel into a critically-acclaimed film of the same name.

Plot Summary

The narrator of *The Hate U Give* is 16-year-old Starr Carter. At the outset of the novel, Starr attends a party in her neighborhood, Garden Heights, which is a primarily Black, lower-income area. A few years before, after witnessing the murder of her friend Natasha in a drive-by shooting, Starr enrolled at Williamson Prep, a private school of mainly White, wealthy students. As a result, Starr feels out of touch with her Garden Heights community. At the party, she reconnects with childhood friend Khalil Harris. When a gang fight at the party results in gunfire, Starr and Khalil leave together in his car. Driving away, they discuss Tupac Shakur's theory of THUG LIFE, an acronym which stands for "The Hate U Give Little Infants Fucks Everybody." However, they are soon pulled over by a White police officer who claims Khalil has a broken taillight and proceeds to order him out of the car to search him. When Khalil moves to ask Starr if she is ok, the officer shoots him multiple times. Starr is the only witness.

Returning to school on Monday, Starr feels uncomfortable around her White boyfriend, Chris, who reminds her of the officer. She realizes that her classmates cannot understand what she went through, reinforcing how different she is from them. Starr's uncle Carlos, who is also a police officer, encourages her to give her statement to the detectives investigating the shooting. Starr goes with her mother Lisa to do so but finds that the detectives frame her interview around Khalil and his connection to gangs and drug dealing. There are no questions about the police officer who shot him. Starr realizes their goal is to twist the story around to blame Khalil for his own murder.

At Khalil's funeral, Starr meets the lawyer and activist April Ofrah who tells her that, as she suspected, the police will not charge the officer with a crime. Starr blames herself for not speaking out for Khalil in the media. At the funeral, King, the leader of the gang the King Lords, places a bandana on Khalil's chest, suggesting he joined the gang. Lack of justice for Khalil's death leads to protests and later riots in Garden Heights. Starr and her family worry about the store owned and operated by Maverick or "Mav," her father. During this time, DeVante, a local boy around Starr's age and a member of the King Lords, comes to Mav for help, as Mav successfully extricated himself from the gang life. Mav agrees to help, allowing DeVante to live with the family. When Mav learns that King wants DeVante dead, he sends DeVante to stay with Starr's Uncle Carlos, a police officer.

Starr also has several altercations with her friend Hailey, who frequently says casually racist things to both her and

Maya, an Asian American friend. Ultimately, Starr cuts off contact with Hailey, who refuses to admit any wrongdoing. Despite King's attempts to intimidate her into silence, Starr testifies before a grand jury, which takes eight weeks to return a decision. They decide not to indict the police officer who shot Khalil. Angry, Starr goes with DeVante, Chris, and her half-brother Seven to the protests, which are reignited by the grand jury decision. They meet April Ofrah there, who persuades Starr to speak to the crowd.

After her speech, Starr throws a tear gas canister back at the police when they start gassing the crowd. The group then goes to Mav's store to get milk to clear the tear gas from their eyes. While there, King and his gang try to burn the store down. Mav arrives just in time to save the group and tells the police that King is to blame, snitching on his old gang buddy. The neighborhood rallies around King, and DeVante agrees to snitch to the police, too, in order to keep King in jail. Even though the store is destroyed, the family resolves to rebuild. Starr feels closer to Chris now that he knows more about her family and neighborhood. She also vows to keep speaking up and being an activist in search of a better future for all.

Chapters 1-5

Part 1: "When It Happens"

Chapter 1 Summary

Starr Carter, the protagonist and narrator, attends a spring break party with her childhood friend, Kenya. The party is in Garden Heights, a fictionalized neighborhood that is primarily made up of Black families with low incomes. Though born and raised in Garden Heights, Starr enrolled at Williamson Prep, a private, mostly White school, six years ago. She has not attended a Garden Heights party in a long time and feels out of place.

Kenya remained Starr's friend in part because they share a brother named Seven. Seven's father is Mav—who is also Starr's father—and his mother is Iesha, Kenya's mother. Meanwhile, Kenya's father is King, the leader of the local gang the King Lords. Mav used to be a part of the gang but left and now owns the neighborhood grocery store.

Kenya encourages Starr to mingle, alternately calling her stuck up for attending the rich White school and telling her how lucky she is to go there. Kenya is upset with a girl named Denasia, who she accuses of flirting with DeVante, a boy Kenya likes.

In the middle of the party, Starr receives a text from Chris, her White boyfriend from Williamson Prep. Upset with him for reasons she does not yet explain, Starr ignores him.

When Kenya leaves Starr alone to go get drinks, she initially feels awkward. Khalil, a childhood friend she hasn't seen in years, approaches her. He asks where she has been, and Starr explains that school and basketball keep her busy. She also challenges Khalil because he is the one who is nowhere to be found recently.

Based on his evasive answer, Starr concludes that he deals drugs, which makes her sad. They continue to catch up, and Khalil mentions the improved health of his mother, a drug addict. He teases her about her love of Drake, the musician, and Starr notices his sneakers. This makes her think of Chris, with whom she often matches limited edition sneakers.

The sound of gunfire interrupts them. Starr looks around for Kenya but cannot see her. Khalil takes her hand and rushes her out of the house and into his car. As Khalil drives to safety Starr texts Kenya and is relieved to learn she is alright.

In the car, Starr and Khalil discuss Tupac Shakur's concept of THUG LIFE, which stands for "The Hate U Give Little Infants Fucks Everybody" (17). They agree that the problems of systemic hatred are still relevant 20 years after Tupac wrote those words. Starr questions Khalil about dealing drugs, and he explains that his grandmother lost her job, his mother is unreliable, and he "got tired of choosing between lights and food" (18).

Seven then texts Starr to make sure she is ok, as he heard about the shooting at the party. Khalil and Starr then share a memory of Natasha; calling themselves The Hood Trio, the three of them were friends as children.

Suddenly, there are lights in the rear-view mirror as a police siren wails.

Chapter 2 Summary

As Khalil pulls the car over, Starr recalls that her parents talked with her when she was young about what to do if the cops pulled her over. They told her to "keep your hands visible. Don't make any sudden moves. Only speak when they speak to you" (20).

Afraid, she asks Khalil if there is anything incriminating in the car, but he assures her there isn't. When the officer approaches and asks for Khalil's license, he asks to know why the officer pulled them over in the first place. At Starr's request, Khalil grudgingly complies with the officer but asks again for the reason behind the traffic stop once he hands over his papers.

The officer, whose badge Starr notices is 115, says Khalil has a broken taillight. When Khalil asks if he will get a ticket, the officer grows hostile and orders him out of the car. He pats Khalil down three times while yelling at Starr not to move. The officer tells Khalil to hold still while he goes back to his car. However, Khalil opens the car door to ask Starr if she is ok. Suddenly, Starr hears gunshots as Khalil's body jerks, hit by the bullets. The officer shoots him three times, and he falls to the ground.

Unable to stop herself, Starr gets out of the car and goes to him. She sees the blood and watches as Khalil dies. Once Khalil passes, Starr realizes the officer has his gun pointed at her now, screaming. She puts her hands up.

Chapter 3 Summary

A short while later, Starr sits in the back of an ambulance while more police officers search Khalil's car. His body is still in the street.

Traumatized, Starr struggles to breathe. However, her father and mother arrive to take her home. On the way, she is sick, and her father pulls the car over long enough to let her vomit.

At home, her parents throw away her bloody clothes while she takes a long bath and scrubs Khalil's blood off of her hands. She then tries to sleep but wakes up several times from nightmares. After one of these, she stares at the ceiling and thinks of Natasha, her best childhood friend. One summer when they were 11, Starr and Natasha went to play in the water from a busted fire hydrant. As they played, there was a drive-by shooting, which resulted in Natasha's death. Starr saw Natasha shot to death and now saw the same thing happen to Khalil.

In the morning, she wants to be alone, but her mother takes her to the kitchen to get food. There is a painting of Black Jesus on a cross in the hallway next to a photo of Malcolm X.

The house is Starr's grandmother's, who lives with Starr's Uncle Carlos in a big house in the suburbs.

Mav and her brothers Seven and Sekani meet her in the kitchen. Seven, who lives with King and his mother Iesha, stayed the previous night to watch Sekani. Despite King's well-known abuse, Seven refuses to leave his other sisters, Kenya and Lyric, alone with him and Iesha.

The family eventually talks about the shooting and expresses disbelief, given that Khalil was so young. Starr tells them that Khalil did not act threatening to the officer. It is agreed that the neighborhood of Garden Heights will not react well when they hear about the shooting. They all agree to tell no one about Starr having been the only witness.

Starr realizes that she "always said that if I saw it happen to somebody, I would have the loudest voice, making sure the world knew what went down. Now I am that person, and I'm too afraid to speak" (35).

Starr wishes she could stay home from school and watch *The Fresh Prince of Bel-Air*, to which she relates her experience at Williamson. She feels like an outsider there and recalls how her home in Garden Heights frightens her Williamson friends.

Starr's mother won't let her stay home, though, and sends her to work at the store with Mav. He does not press her to talk. When they arrive at the small store, Mr. Lewis from the barbershop next store hassles Mav, saying that Mav is late in opening the store.

Regular neighborhood customers filter into the store. A conversation makes Starr think of Chris; Seven and Starr's mother are the only family members who knows Starr is dating him. She worries what her father will do when he finds out her boyfriend is White.

They go across the street to get ribs from Reuben's for lunch. While they wait for their order, they watch a news report about Khalil, but the reporter doesn't even say his name. Back outside, they are stopped as Kenya's father King pulls up in a BMW. He smokes a cigar and has two tear drop tattoos indicating he is responsible for two deaths. He tries to pay for their food, but Starr refuses his money.

Mav comes out of the store and greets King. King tries to get Mav to hold a package for him, but he refuses. When

King gets upset, Mav reminds him that he did three years of jail time to help King out. He also tells King to leave Seven alone.

Chapter 4 Summary

Starr has a nightmare about the deaths of Natasha and Khalil, which frightens her awake. On her way to the kitchen, she hears voices and stops to listen. Her Uncle Carlos, her mother Lisa's brother and a police detective, speaks to Starr's parents about the shooting. Carlos argues that the shooting was not necessarily racially motivated and that Khalil was a drug dealer, which possibly affected the officer's actions.

Furthermore, he knows Officer 115, whom he calls Brian, which surprises Starr. He also tells Lisa that the family should move to a safer neighborhood, which Mav opposes. Finally, he wants Starr to go down to the police station to talk to the detectives, arguing that it will help the case.

Starr accidentally causes the floor to creak, and the adults discover her. In the kitchen, Carlos asks Starr to give a witness statement to the police, assuring her that it will help get justice for Khalil. Based on this reassurance, she agrees.

Carlos leaves, and Lisa goes to bed, leaving Starr and Mav to talk. Starr wonders why her father and Uncle Carlos don't get along. Her father tells her that Carlos never thought he was good enough for his sister Lisa. However, Starr suspects that there is tension because Carlos acted as a father to her and Seven during the three years that Mav was in prison. As a result, Carlos got to experience a lot of firsts with Starr.

Starr wonders aloud if the police truly want justice in the case of Khalil's murder. Her father tells her they need to wait and see.

The next morning, on Sunday, Starr goes with her parents to visit Ms. Rosalie, Khalil's grandmother who took care of him and his younger brother since childhood. She supported Lisa when she was kicked out of the house for getting pregnant, and Starr spent much of her childhood at Rosalie's house.

Brenda, Khalil's mother, isn't there. Starr sits with Rosalie, who is happy to see her. She also reveals that she knows Starr was with Khalil and saw him killed. She is happy at least that a friend was with him. Rosalie also tells Mav that Khalil wanted his help to get out of the drug dealing game. He knew that it would only lead to his arrest or his death.

Chapter 5 Summary

On Monday, Starr gets ready to go back to school after Spring Break. She also plans to talk to the police in the afternoon. Though Starr would prefer to stay home, Lisa makes her go to school. She tells Starr that she can't stop living, even though Khalil is no longer alive.

Once at school, Starr transforms herself into "Williamson Starr," who is a different version of normal Starr in Garden Heights. Williamson Starr can't do things like use slang or seem upset for fear of being stereotyped as "ghetto" or an angry girl. Her only act of individuality is that she always wears dope sneakers and a matching backpack.

Before school starts, she meets up with her friends and fellow basketball teammates in the cafeteria. Among these are Maya and Hailey, her two best friends. Maya, an Asian

American girl, dates Ryan, the only other Black student in their grade. Hailey, who is White, is the self-appointed leader of the trio, and Starr admits that she gives into her a lot.

As the group exchanges Spring Break stories, Starr feels uncomfortable. Her friends traveled to the Bahamas, Taipei, and Disney World. These are all impossible trips for Starr, whose family cannot afford to go on vacations like that. She hopes "none of them ask about my spring break. They went to Taipei, the Bahamas, Harry Potter World. I stayed in the hood and saw a cop kill my friend" (77).

Starr notices a coolness from Hailey, who stopped texting her as much. Hailey also unfollowed Starr's Tumblr account after she reblogged pictures of Emmett Till, a 14-year-old Black boy beaten to death in 1955 for whistling at a White woman. Hailey was mad at Starr for sharing the images, not for what the images portrayed.

On her way to her first class, Starr sees Chris waiting for her. She is still mad at him, but she misses him. Maya and Hailey are protective, but Starr agrees to speak to him. She is upset because Chris tried to pressure her into having sex with him the day before Khalil died, even though she previously told him she wasn't ready.

After apologizing again, Chris attempts to win Starr over by dancing and singing her the theme song from *The Fresh Prince of Bel-Air*, which they both love. It starts to work; Starr has a good time. However, when Chris takes her hand, she suddenly has a flashback of Officer 115 shooting Khalil. She comes to the upsetting realization that Chris reminds her of the White police officer. As she cries, Maya and Hailey assume it is because of something Chris did.

After school, Seven picks up Starr and Sekani and takes them to the clinic where Lisa works. On the way, a police car pulls up behind them at a red light, making Seven and Starr nervous. However, it passes by without incident. They bring Chinese food with them to the clinic, and the family eats together in the break room.

However, they are interrupted by Brenda, Khalil's mother, who enters crying about the death of her son. Lisa is sympathetic, but Starr is indignant because Brenda was never there for Khalil. Her drug habit kept her from being a mother to him.

Lisa gets mad at Starr for mentioning this and yells at her that she has no right to judge, given that Brenda carried and gave birth to Khalil. When Starr brings Brenda some food, she looks at her and "Khalil's eyes stare back at me, and I realize my mom's right. Ms. Brenda is Khalil's momma. Regardless" (92).

Chapters 1-5 Analysis

The events of the first section of the book lay the groundwork for the rest of the story. Crucially, Starr witnesses Khalil's murder by Officer 115 and sees how both the authorities and members of her Garden Heights community handle this crime.

However, even before Khalil is shot, the author explores issues of systemic racism in American culture, which is a major theme. When the officer pulls them over, Starr remembers everything her parents taught her about how to survive such an occurrence. While most White people would not think much of a traffic stop, Starr is immediately afraid. Additionally, both she and Khalil know that they did not break any driving laws—the officer pulled them over because they were Black. This is proven in Officer 115's suspicious treatment of Khalil and, ultimately, in his decision to shoot and kill him. Although Carlos argues that Khalil's activity as a drug dealer may have influenced the officer's decision-making, there is nothing to indicate that the officer was aware of Khalil's involvement in the drug trade. In any case, even if the officer somehow knew of Khalil's involvement—which, again, is unlikely—that would not justify killing him. All of this supports Starr's contention that the shooting was racially-motivated.

Starr and the rest of the characters spend the rest of the book struggling to understand and then fight against this system of ingrained racism in the Garden Heights police department and society in general. Although the book exists firmly within the framework of young adult, coming-of-age fiction, the author uses that framework to spark discussions about police brutality and the Black Lives Matter movement in environments where they may not otherwise be explored. According to Harvard's Kennedy School of Government Professor Khalil Muhammad, "The book—and to some degree the movie—has been read and will be read by students in all-White spaces, where otherwise the urgency of these issues has not affected them personally." (Weissman, Elena. "State violence and racial justice: 'The Hate U Give' could sear on screen." *Christian Science Monitor*. 20 Mar. 2019. https://www.csmonitor.com/The-Culture/Movies/2018/1005/State-violence-and-racial-justice-The-Hate-U-Give-could-sear-on-screens.)

Additionally, the author introduces Tupac's idea of "T.H.U.G. L.I.F.E.". This acronym stands for "The Hate U Give Little Infants Fucks Everybody" (17). As Starr and Khalil discuss, Tupac used it to describe the cyclical nature of hate and the damage done by systems designed around hatred. Khalil's murder in large part happens because Officer 115 exists as part of a racially discriminatory justice system that encourages the dehumanization of minorities. This hatred is not always overt, but it results in officers like 115 immediately suspecting the worst of people based on the color of their skin. It leads to harassment, assumptions, and, ultimately, the shooting of an innocent unarmed Black boy. In turn, the community is mobilized by hatred of the police due to the murder, as the cycle of hatred continues. This is not to draw a false dichotomy between racist police brutality and community hostilities toward the police; after all, the police operate with the power of the state behind them. Nevertheless, the author acknowledges through her narrative the cyclical nature of hostilities between communities and police departments.

This first section also introduces one of Starr's central conflicts: dealing with two very different sides of her life. She has her home life in Garden Heights which, though often dysfunctional and dangerous, is ultimately loving. On the other hand, she has her life at Williamson, which is safe and normal but still difficult navigate emotionally. Starr must be careful not to let her two personas overlap, for fear of being singled out as either too "ghetto" by her Williamson friends or too stuck-up by her Garden Heights friends. This is a constant source of stress for Starr, especially as her worlds start to collide.

Chapters 6-10

Chapter 6 Summary

Starr goes to the police station with her mother to give her statement to the detectives. She is nervous and frightened when she walks in and sees so many officers with guns.

They meet Uncle Carlos, and Lisa insists on going with Starr when she talks to the detectives on the case.

Carlos takes them to a room with a table and chairs. Two cops, Detective Gomez and Detective Wilkes, greet them. Detective Gomez, a Latina woman, asks most of the questions. She asks Starr how long she knew Khalil and asks for the story of "the incident." Starr explains what happened, being careful not to say anything that would make it seem like the shooting was Khalil's fault.

Several times, Gomez tries to imply that Khalil resisted the officer or acted suspiciously, which Starr denies. Starr is clear that the officer harassed Khalil and that when he moved, his intent was to ask her if she was ok.

Gomez then asks if Khalil sold narcotics, a question which confuses Starr, given that it has nothing to do with the shooting. She honestly tells Gomez that while Khalil never told her about his involvement in the drug trade, she heard about it from the others. Gomez then asks if he was involved with the King Lords or Garden Disciples, rival gangs. Starr doesn't know.

After the short interview, Starr and her mother leave, but they both know "this is gonna be some bullshit" (103).

Chapter 7 Summary

Khalil's funeral is set for Friday, a week after he died. Starr notices that the news media calls him a suspected drug dealer every time they mention his name.

At school on Thursday, Starr is in gym class with Hailey and Maya after lunch. As Hailey watches some of the class playing basketball, she is annoyed by the girls' team perceived lack of effort. She then decides that they will play 3 vs. 3 with the boys, without even asking if Starr and Maya even want to participate.

Chris joins the other team and takes the position guarding Starr. For a minute, Starr enjoys herself because "no matter what's going on, when Hailey, Maya, and I play together, it's rhythm, chemistry and skill rolled into a ball of amazingness" (109).

However, Chris distracts her by being in close physical proximity to her. Distracted by Chris's physical proximity to her and the realization that she misses him, Starr misses several opportunities to steal the ball, angering Hailey, who tells her to pretend the ball is fried chicken so she'll stay on it.

Shocked at Hailey's racist comment, Starr leaves the court abruptly. Maya and Hailey follow her, and Starr tells Maya that she is upset about the ugly invocation of a racist stereotype. Hailey then gets mad at Starr for implying that she is racist. Starr maintains that "you can say something racist and not be a racist!" (112).

Hailey deflects by asking about the drug dealer shot in Starr's neighborhood. Worried about how her friends and school will see her if they associate her with the "drug dealer" on the news, Starr denies knowing Khalil at all, which she views as a betrayal. Hailey then assumes Starr is upset about the anniversary of Natasha's death; the two of them initially bonded because Hailey lost her mother around a similar time.

Starr goes to the office and calls Uncle Carlos to come pick her up from school. He always comes to get her when she calls about "feminine problems" (116).

They stop for frozen yogurt on the way, and Carlos calls Lisa to tell her that he picked up Starr. Carlos then presses Starr about what is really the matter. She tells him that she isn't sure she should go to the funeral the next day, given that she hadn't seen Khalil in months. When Starr asks Carlos if he is friends with Officer 115, he says they are just colleagues. She then asks if Carlos would have shot Khalil in the same circumstances, a question he cannot answer. Finally, she tells Carlos that the officer pointed his gun at her, too. This upsets him and her hugs her, apologizing.

Chapter 8 Summary

At the funeral, Pastor Eldridge greets them and expresses his sympathies for Starr, as Ms. Rosalie told him she was the witness. As Starr waits in line to pay her respects to Khalil in his coffin, she notes how his body looks like a mannequin. She remembers thinking the same thing about Natasha and realizes she is the only one left of the Hood Trio.

The service starts, the Pastor gives the eulogy, and the congregations sings to celebrate Khalil's life and return to heaven. Then, several of Khalil's classmates give a presentation about him, which makes Starr feel sad because she was not as good a friend to him as they were.

Next, April Ofrah, who introduces herself as an attorney working for the Just Us for Justice foundation, speaks. She tells the congregation that she heard that the police decided not to press charges against Officer 115. She also tells them that Khalil was unarmed when he was shot. She says her foundation won't give up in its pursuit of justice for him.

As the funeral ends, King arrives with Seven's mother
Iesha on his arm, which causes tension between Mav and
Lisa. Seven was born when Mav and Lisa had a fight, so he
slept with King's girl. King walks up to Khalil and lays a
gray bandana on his chest, signaling that he had been a
King Lord. This upsets Ms. Rosalie, who throws the
bandana away. Later, she thanks Starr for coming, as she
knows that Starr meant a lot to Khalil.

Outside as they leave the church, they see protestors
holding signs. April Ofrah comes over to speak to Starr,
telling her that she wants to help make sure her side of the
story is heard without anyone exploiting her. She gives her
a business card and says to call when she's ready.
However, Starr doesn't know if she'll ever be ready to
speak.

Chapter 9 Summary

That night, Mav decides to stay over at the store because he
worries the protests may turn into riots in Garden Heights.
At home, the rest of the family hears gunshots and eats
dinner on the floor of the den to stay safe. They watch the
news and see protestors on Magnolia Avenue. When the
cops spray the crowd with tear gas, everyone runs. Images
of looting car-fires fill the television screen. Starr
concludes, "my neighborhood is a war zone" (139).

Chris texts both Hailey and Maya call to make sure Starr is
ok. Lisa checks in on the neighbors, and everything
remains quiet on their street. Mav comes home and says the
riots are confined to the east side of the neighborhood,
away from them and the store.

Starr goes to bed and has a nightmare about Natasha. With
the riots having died down, Seven wakes her up in the

morning and talks her into playing basketball in the park. Still, there is smoke in the air and they see cop cars on the streets.

At the park, Starr dominates the game of basketball until two Garden Disciple gang members approach them. They ask if Seven is a King Lord, which he is not, and then try to mug them. However, a boy sitting on the merry-go-round watching the game comes up and tells them the park is King territory. He indicates two nearby King Lords in a car. The rival gang members leave.

The boy introduces himself; he is DeVante, the boy that Kenya was upset about at the party before Khalil's death. For this reason, Starr is cool toward him when he flirts with her. Suddenly, Mav screeches up in his Tahoe and yells at Seven and Starr for leaving the house, embarrassing them in front of DeVante and the other nearby King Lords. He takes them home, where Lisa also yells at them for going out without telling anyone the day after a riot. She then confiscates their phones and sends them to Uncle Carlos's house for the day.

Once on the freeway, Lisa sees Starr is upset and tells her that when she was born, she could not breathe, even though Lisa did everything right during her pregnancy. She said one of the nurses told her "sometimes you can do everything right and things will still go wrong. The key is to never stop doing what's right" (154).

They reach Uncle Carlos's house, which is near where Maya and Chris live, but Starr is grounded and thus forbidden to see them. As Carlos cooks food on the grill, his wife Pam greets everyone warmly. Nana, Lisa's mother, pulls them aside to say she wants to return to live in Garden Heights because she doesn't like Pam.

Later, Chris comes over because he saw their car arrive. He apologizes to Starr about pressuring her into having sex. Starr also apologizes for being distant, telling him he wouldn't understand. Hurt by this, Chris presses her until she admits that the reason he wouldn't understand is because he is White. Chris tries to say he doesn't care about race, but Starr informs him that she has to care about it because it affects her whole life. Chris admits she is right, he doesn't understand. He tells her he misses her, though.

Talking with him, Starr starts to feel normal again. She decides she can't jeopardize that feeling by telling him the truth about being a witness that night.

Chapter 10 Summary

At sundown, the riots start again, causing Starr and Seven to spend the night at Carlos's house. On the way home the next day, they pass through a police roadblock, which scares Starr. She panics and grips the door handle all the way through. They pass through without incident and Lisa tells her it's all fine. But Starr realizes "her words used to have power. If she said it was fine, it was fine. But after you've held two people as they took their last breaths, words like that don't mean shit anymore" (165).

When they get home, Mav decides to take Starr with him to the warehouse to replenish the store. On the way, they talk about Harry Potter and listen to Tupac. As they discuss T.H.U.G. L.I.F.E., Starr decides that it refers to how society treats any oppressed group; they are hated but also feared.

Mav points out that Khalil had little choice in becoming a drug dealer. He needed money and had no opportunities for work elsewhere. He also explains that while drugs destroy communities like Garden Heights, the drugs come from elsewhere and are controlled by the wealthy. The hate Tupac referred to is therefore the system that is designed against oppressed groups, like the Black community in Garden Heights.

T.H.U.G. L.I.F.E. also applies to the riots, because the hate given to the community explodes into violence and anger in a vicious cycle that "fucks everyone" (171). They agree that nothing will change if everyone is silent. Starr concludes that she should therefore speak out, and Mav agrees.

As they stock the shelves of the story, DeVante arrives and pretends he wants to buy something. However, he is really there to hide from King, who ordered him to kill the guys who shot DeVante's brother on the night of the Spring Break party. Starr realizes that was the party she attended before Khalil's murder.

DeVante doesn't want to kill anyone and furthermore wants out of the King Lords for good. Although Mav got out, he explains that he only escaped because he took the fall when the police arrested him and King for moving weapons. King let him out of the gang because he was grateful. However, this rarely happens. Usually, being in a gang is for life.

Still, DeVante wants out because he wants to stay alive. Mav agrees to help him. He says he can work in the store to start. Starr teaches him how to use the price gun and realizes that she possibly misjudged him before.

That night, DeVante stays with the Carters, which upsets Lisa, because King would be mad if he knew. She says she wants to move to a safer neighborhood, whether Mav comes or not. Starr overhears this argument and worries for her parents' safety.

Chapters 6-10 Analysis

In this section, Starr confronts additional examples of systemic racism and its seeming acceptance by American society at large. First, when she gives her statement to the police, the entire interview is structured to suggest that Khalil did something to justify Officer 115 murdering him. Detective Gomez immediately gives the police officer the benefit of the doubt that he was correct in his actions, while assuming Khalil did something wrong. Starr recognizes this and knows that it is very unlikely Khalil will get justice; after all, she lived her whole life dealing with these systems and saw cops get away with shooting Black kids before. The interview reflects the extent to which power structures within police departments, combined with the extraordinary discretion given to individual officers and detectives, hampers good-faith efforts to uncover the truth of a crime.

On a more personal level, Starr's friend Hailey makes a racist remark to her during gym class. Starr is upset and confronts Hailey, but rather than realize her casually offensive behavior – whether she intended to be racist or not – Hailey grows defensive. She refuses to believe she said anything wrong and, in fact, wants Starr to apologize to her for thinking it was racially motivated. Hailey, who is from a wealthy White family, immediately assumes a position of power and attempts to force Starr, a minority, to accept racist language as part of a larger system of racism. For even calling attention to the problem that disadvantages her, Starr is attacked. This is consistent with sociological theories of White fragility, which state that White society often views accusations of racism as more offensive than actual racism. This is said to stem from an inability on the part of many White Americans to acknowledge racist actions and statements outside the context of the overt and often violent bigotry exercised by self-affiliated White supremacists. Starr implies this when, in exasperation, she tells Hailey, "you can say something racist and not be a racist!" (112).

This encounter is also symbolic of the protests that occur in response to Khalil's murder. The protestors call out the injustice of the shooting, but the police respond to them as if they are a dangerous threat. This is complicated by the fact that the protests become riots involving the gangs in Garden Heights. Ultimately, however, the message is the same. The oppressive system moves swiftly to say that the disenfranchised minorities should quietly accept the system that disadvantages them. This narrative is reinforced by the media. News reporters initially do not mention Khalil by name, and when they finally do, they invariably refer to Khalil as a drug dealer. According to *The New Jim Crow* author Michelle Alexander, the news media has a long and ugly legacy of dehumanizing Black men as criminals in the public imagination in this manner. (Alexander, Michelle. *The New Jim Crow: Mass Incarceration in the Age of Colorblindness*. New York: New York Press. 2012.) This legacy is also reflected in the news reports' tendency to focus on images of looting and fires set by protestors, rather than on the act of injustice that sparked the protests.

Interestingly, Starr rarely refers to Officer 115 by his name, even though she learns it from Carlos. This may reflect the extent to which Officer 115, aside from whatever personal biases he possesses, is a reflection of a faceless organization—the police—and the racist outcomes the organization creates by virtue of its structure. Thus, Officer 115 is seen not as a "bad apple," but as a cog in a vast superstructure of racial injustice.

The character of Chris also serves to highlight the more insidious aspects of systemic racism. Chris is not a racist; he is a White character who advocates for minority communities. However, though he is incredibly well-intentioned, he internalizes certain ideas about race due to his upbringing as a privileged White male. For example, he tells Starr that race doesn't matter to him, meaning this as a good thing.

But, as Starr explains to him, she does not have the luxury of ignoring issues of race because they directly affect her life every day, sometimes in deadly ways. Thus, Chris must come to understand that the ability to ignore race is a privilege, one that hurts the disadvantaged communities he intends to help.

The theme of T.H.U.G. L.I.F.E. recurs, as Starr discusses it with her father, Mav. She sees how dangerous the cyclical nature of hate can be and how difficult it is to break, especially when the systems in place are designed to block non-violent avenues for justice for some groups.

Interestingly, the gang dynamics established in this section have a lot in common with the dynamics of the justice system that Starr faces. The gang rules that govern the neighborhood are also designed to favor the powerful and to keep the less powerful from speaking out or fighting for justice. King controls the neighborhood via the King Lords, and everyone is expected to accept his whims, including Mav, despite having escaped the gang life.

Chapter 11 Summary

On Monday, Hailey's older brother Remy organizes a protest at school. Although they protest Khalil's death, the real reason for the demonstration is to get out of class. This infuriates Starr because "they're so damn excited about getting a day off. Khalil's in a grave. He can't get a day off from that shit. I live it every single day too" (183).

Five minutes into the first class, the kids start to chant, "Justice for Khalil" and walk out of the classroom. Hailey and Maya go with them, but Starr doesn't move. Guessing that she knew Khalil, Chris doesn't leave either. She doesn't tell him that she was a witness and asks the teacher to continue with the lesson to distract her.

Throughout the day, most of the classes are empty except for Starr, Chris, and sometimes another person or two. Many of them apologize to Starr for the protest, making her feel like they think "I'm the official representative of the black race and they owe me an explanation. I think I understand, though. If I sit out a protest, I'm making a statement, but if they sit out a protest, they look racist" (186).

After school, Starr goes to the store with Seven and Sekani. Due to the unrest, a curfew starts at nine o'clock in the evening. Outside, two cops interview Mr. Lewis about the King Lords, who allegedly jumped a couple of their colleagues. Mr. Lewis names King as the one who ordered the hit, committing the cardinal sin of snitching on live TV. However, he tells them that he isn't scared of the King Lords because he's survived worse. He also tells Mav that by refusing to snitch on King, Mav is still under his control.

As their talk grows heated, two police officers stop to see what the argument is about. Despite Mr. Lewis's insistence that it was just a discussion, the police ask for Mav's ID. When they recognize the last name "Carter," they realize that he is the father of the witness to the shooting. The cops order Mav to get on the ground. He complies and they search him three times. Onlookers from the neighborhood witness this and refuse to follow the cops' orders to move along.

After the cops leave, they all go into the store where Kenya and DeVante are. Mav goes into his office and is visibly angry. Mr. Lewis and a neighborhood man named Tim accompany him. They tell him that the whole neighborhood knows that Starr was the witness because someone saw Mav and Lisa pick her up from the scene. Kenya asks why Starr continues to keep quit if she was the witness, adding that she should go on TV. Starr then talks to her father, who tells her not to be scared. No matter what, if she talks or if she protects herself and stays silent, he has her back.

Chapter 12 Summary

That afternoon, tanks arrive in the neighborhood, as if the police expect to go to war against the protestors. At home, Mav asks Starr for her old laptop, which he wants to repurpose for DeVante. While retrieving it, she gets on Tumblr and uploads pictures of Khalil from when they were children. She does not put her name on the posts, but hundreds of people like and reblog the images.

The District Attorney calls to say that she wants to meet with Starr. She agrees, but the family decides that she should talk to April Ofrah first. Starr then asks her mother for a day off school; she agrees.

Lisa and Mav take Starr to see April Ofrah at the Just Us for Justice headquarters, located in an old Taco Bell. April explains the work the group to win justice for Khalil's murder. She then explains that the DA wants her to testify to a grand jury, which will ultimately decide if Officer 115 will be charged with any crime.

Starr is concerned by news reports that Khalil had a gun, which he didn't. April explains it was his hairbrush that the officer claimed looked like a gun. She then tells the family that Officer 115's father is plans to give an interview on TV. Starr realizes that the father will try to make the officer look like the victim, not Khalil, and that "the only way people will know his side of the story is if I speak out" (218).

April says she will secure Starr an interview, but there will be no names, and they will disguise her voice to protect her privacy.

Chapter 13 Summary

At the store, Mr. Lewis suffers injuries at the hands of King Lords. He is hurt but he refuses to go to the hospital, instead bragging that it took five of them to bring him down. He also says that the gang members didn't want to kill him—they want to kill DeVante.

Furious, Mav demands to know the full story as to why DeVante is in hiding. He admits that he stole $5,000 from King, which he used to get his family out of the neighborhood and to a safer place. Though angry, Mav understands. He says they need to get DeVante out of their house. Instead, they take him to Carlos. When they arrive, Starr notes that her uncle's knuckles are bruised. DeVante is skeptical of Carlos at first, because he is a cop. However, he is impressed by the size of his house and asks how Carlos got it. Carlos tells the family that he is on leave from the police station.

Meanwhile, Chris comes to the door, having seen the car arrive. Mav wants to know who he is, and Starr musters the courage to tell him that Chris is her boyfriend. Mav is furious at the news that her boyfriend is White, especially when he finds out that everyone else in the family knew, including Carlos. Lisa takes Mav outside to cool down, and Chris asks about DeVante, who also makes a remark about Starr dating a White boy. Outside, they can hear her parents arguing about Chris. Chris then asks if this is a "black thing" he wouldn't understand (230). Starr explains that race isn't a Black thing and points out that he and his parents discussed the fact that his girlfriend was Black, too.

Outside, Lisa and Mav argue about leaving Garden Heights altogether. Lisa is upset that Mav got DeVante out but won't move his own children out of danger. Angry, Mav storms in, tells Starr they will talk later, and leaves. Obviously nervous, Chris stays by Starr's side. Once they are alone, they kiss but are caught by Lisa. Embarrassed, Chris leaves. Lisa asks Starr if she takes her birth control.

DeVante returns and asks Starr why she doesn't date a Garden Heights boy. He then says that Khalil talked to him about Starr a lot. She assumes they knew each other because they were both King Lords, but DeVante explains that Khalil never become a King Lord, even though King asked him to join. King only came to the funeral and laid the bandana on Khalil to save face.

He also explains that Khalil started selling drugs because his mother stole from King, and he had to pay him back.

Hearing all of this, Starr is upset that she thought the worst of Khalil, just like so many people had.

DeVante admits that while he is a "thug" unlike Khalil, the King Lords offered him and his brother the only family they ever knew. Now his brother is dead, which is why he wanted to save the rest of his family.

Chapter 14 Summary

Starr walks to Maya's house and sees Hailey's car in the driveway. Mrs. Yang lets her in, and Maya runs downstairs to hug her. They go upstairs to Maya's room, and Starr awkwardly greets Hailey. When Starr asks about the protest at school, Hailey is defensive. Maya understands why Starr is upset and apologizes for using the protest as a way to cut class, but Hailey refuses to apologize. Instead, she once again wants Starr to apologize to *her* for calling her a racist.

Starr will not apologize for how she felt. Unable to agree, they decide to watch TV. As they flip through channels, they land on the interview with Officer 115's father. He says his son, a 16-year veteran of the force, feared for his life. He worked in Garden Heights all that time and only wanted to make a difference in the notoriously dangerous neighborhood. Starr thinks about how "slave masters thought they were making a difference in people's lives, too" (245).

The father tells an exaggerated version of events, claiming that the officer pulled them over for speeding and that Starr and Khalil cursed at him. The entire interview makes the two of them out to be monsters, while Officer 115 seems like a victim; as a result, Starr struggles not to cry. The father says his son faced backlash and is afraid to go to the store. He suffered physical and verbal attacks. Hearing this,

Starr realizes that Uncle Carlos's knuckles were bruised because he hit 115, which is why he is on leave.

When the interview ends, Hailey expresses sympathy for the family on TV. Starr is shocked, but Hailey says that Officer 115's life matters, too. Furious, Starr starts to leave, but Maya stops her. Starr asks Hailey why she unfollowed her on Tumblr after she posted the Emmett Till picture. Again, Hailey grows defensive, saying that Starr implied she is racist again. Starr says she never mentioned race. Hailey storms out, adding that she doesn't like who Starr is anymore.

Maya says that Hailey is lying and that she unfollowed Starr because of all the "black stuff" on her Tumblr (250). She says it's not the first time Hailey was casually racist. She tells Starr about an incident during freshman year when Hailey asked Maya if her family eats cat because they are Asian. Hailey laughed like it was a joke, and so Maya had laughed too out of obligation. Together, they decide that they can't let Hailey get away with saying things like that anymore. They decide to form a "minority alliance" (252).

Walking home later, Starr meets Uncle Carlos on the stoop of his house as he drinks a beer, which is unusual for him given that his mother was an alcoholic. He tells Starr that he punched Officer 115 for pointing his gun at her. He also feels bad about what he said previously about Khalil and that "I hate that I let myself fall into that mindset of trying to rationalize his death. And at the end of the day, you don't kill someone for opening a car door" (256).

He tells Starr that he would not have killed Khalil. Starr hugs him and tries not to cry.

Chapter 15 Summary

Before they go to the DA's office the next morning, Lisa takes Starr to IHOP, just like she used to before Sekani was born. Starr then tells her about Hailey, which does not surprise her mother. She explains how Hailey always pushed Starr and Maya around and that the two of them always fell over themselves to please her. Starr doesn't know if she can forgive Hailey, and Lisa tells her: "you have to decide if the relationship is worth salvaging. Make a list of the good stuff, then make a list of the bad stuff. If one outweighs the other, then you know what you gotta do" (264). She says that she used this method when she went back to Mav after he slept with Iesha. Her love was bigger than his mistake.

Later, District Attorney Karen Monroe and April Ofrah meet them at the DA's office. After the DA explains the grand jury process, Starr tells her the story of Khalil's murder. Near the end, she vomits and cries.

After the meeting, Starr accompanies Mav to the store. While there, they talk about Chris. Mav explains his dislike of Chris. He worries that Starr chose him because Mav didn't set a good example of what a Black man should be. Starr denies this, telling him that he was a good example of a man, period.

King pulls up to the store and asks Mav where DeVante is. Mav denies any knowledge. King then says that he knows that Starr is the witness and doesn't want her saying too much about Khalil's involvement with drugs, since it will lead back to King. Following a tense standoff between him and Mav, King leaves.

After dinner that night, Lisa reveals that she interviewed for a much better paying job at Markham Memorial Hospital. Mav tells her that they will go look for a new house away from Garden Heights before her next interview.

Although the family is happy about this news, Seven tells Starr that he won't leave Garden Heights with the rest of them. Rather than go away to college as planned, he will stay and go to community college to protect his sisters, Kenya and Lyric, and his mother Iesha.

Chapters 11-15 Analysis

Starr continues to confront issues of systemic racism and its effects. First, the students at Williamson stage a protest against Khalil's death; however, the true motive is simply to cut class, as the kids don't really care about the shooting. The majority-White, majority-wealthy community at school co-opts the very serious protests against murder for their own gain. This not only makes a mockery of Khalil's death but undercuts the power of the real protests.

Elsewhere, Officer 115's father gives an interview on the local news intended to garner sympathy for his son. He constructs the entire speech to skew the events, making Khalil out to be a "thug" and a dangerous drug dealer, while describing the police officer as a good man who only wanted to help. In this speech, the father characterizes the entirety of Garden Heights as a dangerous place full of gangs and drug dealers. Although the father never overtly calls it a Black neighborhood, the implication is clear. This is a prime example of dog whistle politics, which appeals to racist beliefs without explicitly mentioning race.

Additionally, Hailey's reaction to this interview is to express immediate sympathy for Officer 115, even though she showed none for Khalil. Her conditioning in White privilege immediately predisposes her to agree with the systemically racist system, rather than with the actual victims.

It is also revealed in this section that Hailey—and, given the character's position as a stand-in for privileged White Americans, much of the rest of society—is casually racist toward both the Black community and the Asian American community. Maya reveals examples of racism she faced due to her Asian heritage. Starr and Maya form an alliance and pledge to help one another fight back against racism of all kinds.

Finally, in this section, Starr decides that she must speak out on Khalil's behalf. She recognizes that the system works by only telling one side of the story—the side of the powerful. Although there are still many obstacles in her way, she decides that she has a duty to bear witness on Khalil's behalf so that the media, the law, and society at large do not dismiss him as a drug dealer whose murder means nothing.

Chapters 16-19

Part 2: "Five Weeks After It"

Chapter 16 Summary

April Ofrah secures Starr an interview with a local news station. The whole family accompanies her to the station. There, a producer calls Starr brave, but she doesn't feel like it. Her interviewer is Diane Carey, a local reporter Starr watched with her grandmother for years. After recording some B-roll footage of them walking around, Diane and Starr sit down. She asks Starr who Khalil was to her. Starr says that he was just a kid and explains why he started selling drugs. Even though she knows King will watch the segment, Starr tells Diane that Khalil sold drugs to pay back the biggest drug dealer in the neighborhood. She doesn't name King, concluding that "it's dry snitching, but it's still snitching" (288).

Starr tells Diane that the media portrayal of Khalil annoys her, because it's as if news reporters charged him with his own murder. She explains that he opened the car door to ask if she was ok when Officer 115 shot him. She also says that the officer pointed his gun at her, which no one but Carlos knew before.

She says while she isn't afraid of the cops, she wishes that they wouldn't make so many assumptions about Black people. Officer 115's assumption that she and Khalil were up to no good led to his murder. When Diane asks what Starr would say to Officer 115 if he was there, she replies, "I'd ask him if he wished he shot me too" (290).

Chapter 17 Summary

When the interview airs, it is one of the most-watched segments in the network's history. Starr even hears that an anonymous millionaire wants to pay her college tuition after seeing it. Kenya texts Starr her grudging approval but adds that King is mad about the dry snitching.

On Saturday, on the way to the prom, Chris is moody and distant. Once they arrive, he goes off to talk to someone while Starr meets up with Maya. Neither girl is on speaking terms with Hailey, though Maya confronted her about the cat question. Hailey told her to get over it because it was a joke. They dance together without either of their boyfriends. Hailey comes in with her date but avoids them.

Finally, Chris comes over to ask Starr if she wants a picture. Annoyed with his behavior, she says no and asks why it feels like he doesn't want to be there. When he doesn't answer, Starr storms out to sit in their car. Chris follows and says he's mad she didn't tell him that she was the witness to the shooting. He recognized her in the interview, even though they blurred her face and distorted the sound. Starr resents that he is upset because she didn't tell him about one of the worst nights of her life. She tells him that she saw two people die, a revelation she never shared with Chris. He believes that she doesn't trust him enough to tell him. Starr admits that this is true—she didn't trust that he would not see her as "ghetto" if he knew everything. He asks her to let him in, emotionally.

Starr cries and tells him about Natasha's death and how her family used to live in a one-bedroom apartment in the projects. All the details come out about how terrible the conditions were because her father couldn't get a job because he was an ex-con. She then talks about Khalil, who had been her first kiss, and whose mother was a crack addict whose decisions more or less forced him into dealing. Starr blames herself for not being there for Khalil. She tells Chris that he was her "normal" through everything, which is another reason she didn't told him everything. He holds her while she cries.

When she finishes, they kiss and Chris tells her that he loves her.

Chapter 18 Summary

On Sunday, the family visits their new house in a nice neighborhood. Lisa got the new job at Markham, allowing them to afford this new home. Their parents tell them that they will move once summer break starts at school. Starr then reveals that Seven does not plan to go away to college. This upsets Mav, who doesn't want Seven to miss opportunities.

They go home and watch a basketball game between Cleveland and Chicago. In the second quarter, gunshots ring out. They all get to the floor and hear tires squeal. The assailants shot through the front window and also threw a brick. They call Carlos while the neighbors check in to make sure everything is ok. Carlos arrives and finds that Mav called the Cedar Grove King Lords, who are in a feud with the local King Lords. They agree to guard the house.

While everyone suspects that King is responsible for the attempt intimidate Starr against testifying, they admit the cops could also be responsible. Starr tries to tell everyone that testifying isn't worth it. However, Mav convinces her that she should, citing Malcolm X and Black Panthers quotes. Angry that Mav enlisted gang members to protect the house, Carlos storms out.

Chapter 19 Summary

The next morning, the Cedar Grove King Lords accompany the family to the courthouse. Starr remembers going there for Mav's trial when she was little. Outside, protestors kneel on the courthouse lawn with signs about Khalil and the shooting.

Inside, Lisa tells Starr she is brave, which she refutes. In response, Lisa tells her that "brave doesn't mean you're not scared […] it means you go on even though you're scared" (331).

Starr is led into the grand jury room and seated at a table with a microphone that records her voice but doesn't amplify sound. She tells the grand jury the same story she already told several times. This time, she feels the weight of the responsibility on her shoulders and rises to the challenge. She straightens up and speaks.

Chapters 16-19 Analysis

In this section, Starr gives voice to the injustices she and the Black community experience by giving a televised interview. She points out directly the racism that led to Officer 115 pulling her and Khalil over and ultimately shooting him. In the same interview, she speaks out indirectly against the gang system in Garden Heights, alluding to King as another major source of injustice in Khalil's life. As a result, both King and the police turn against her, making Starr feel unsafe and almost preventing her from testifying. However, her commitment to justice for Khalil ultimately prevails. Starr's realization and ultimate embrace of her responsible in the fight for racial justice make up the dominant character arc of the narrative.

Starr's journey with Chris as a White advocate also continues in this section, as they have a disagreement when he learns she was the witness. Chris is upset that he wasn't told while Starr is upset that he expects her to tell him these things. However, Chris wants to understand her experience—her whole true experience—and Starr realizes that he cannot know if she doesn't open up to him. Again, the idea that speaking out is necessary to end discriminatory systems and undo the harm caused by them is key. She does this again by testifying to the grand jury.

Finally, the Carter family intends to move away from Garden Heights in this section. There is some struggle to remain connected to the community and not abandon it, but ultimately, they are able to reconcile the two worlds. This mirrors Starr's struggle to reconcile her life in Garden Heights with her life at Williamson.

Chapters 20-21

Part 3: "Eight Weeks After It"

Chapter 20 Summary

Starr testified in front of the grand jury for three hours, giving answers to lots of specific questions. Two weeks pass, and no one knows when they will get an answer regarding a possible grand jury indictment of Officer 115.

When Starr arrives at school, she sees Maya and Hailey talking. Hailey confronts Starr, calling her a liar. She figured out that Starr knew Khalil and that both Maya and Hailey met him at Starr's 12th birthday party. Hailey wants an explanation and an apology.

Instead, Maya and Starr confront her about her racist behavior. She gets defensive, telling them that they should both get over it. She tells Starr to get over Khalil's death because he was a drug dealer, so it was only a matter of time before he died. When she says "the cop probably did everyone a favor. One less drug dealer," Starr punches her in the side of the face (341).

Hailey's brother Remy steps in to try to stop Starr, but Seven gets involved and fights Remy. Security guards break up the fight, and both Starr and Seven are sent home. Hailey's father demanded Starr's expulsion, but the headmaster suspends Starr instead.

Lisa is mad at Starr and Seven for resorting to violence just like "They" expect, adding "They with a capital T. There's

Them and then there's Us. Sometimes They look like Us and don't realize They are Us" (343).

At home, they find Mav in a meeting with the Cedar Grove King Lords and the Garden Disciples—usually rival gangs. He wants them to control the riots that will inevitably break out if the grand jury decides not to indict Officer 115. Both sides agree.

Part 4: "Ten Weeks After It"

Chapter 21 Summary

Four weeks after Starr's testimony, there is still no grand jury decision. Over Memorial Day weekend, they have a party to celebrate Seven's birthday and his graduation. At the party, Kenya flirts with DeVante even though her father, King, wants him dead.

Chris and Maya join the party, and Starr worries about how to behave as her two worlds collide. Kenya meets Chris for the first time, and Maya tells her about Starr's fight, which Kenya appreciates. Lisa gets everyone to dance, and Starr starts to relax.

Later, while Starr is inside, the phone rings. It's the guard at the front gate, who tells them that Iesha is outside asking to be let in. Seven invited his grandmother to come, and Iesha came along. He lets her in after DeVante hides.

Iesha is upset that Seven didn't invite her to his birthday. Seven gets mad at her when she makes a scene about it. He yells at her, saying that she never knows how to act and calling her a bad mother. He accuses her of choosing King over her own children and says that Lisa has been more of a mother to him than her. Iesha accuses Mav and Lisa of turning Seven against her, saying she can't wait for King to "fuck y'all up for letting that girl snitch on him on TV" (365). She leaves.

Seven cries, but Starr understands why Iesha might be afraid to leave King. Kenya comes into the house looking for her brother, and Starr finally confronts her about always calling him her brother instead of their brother. Kenya does not respond.

They all go back outside for cake and Mav makes a speech for Seven's birthday. He tells him that he is proud of him and that he is going to do great things.

Chapters 20-21 Analysis

In this section, Hailey's ingrained racism finally boils over in a confrontation with Starr. Again, she refuses to apologize for or even recognize the casual racism in her language or her ideas. Instead, she echoes the sentiment implied by the police and the media since Khalil's death: that it's better this way because there is one less drug dealer on the street. This kind of justification rightfully infuriates Starr and she resorts to violence. This is her first step in understanding why the Garden Heights community riots. Additionally, Hailey's reaction is consistent with larger societal efforts that work to dehumanize Black men and women, devaluing their lives. Beating back against this narrative lies at the heart of the Black Lives Matter movement and is one of the driving forces behind the author's decision to write *The Hate U Give*.

Also in this section, Seven fights back against the gang system in Garden Heights. As the son of a former gang member and King's girlfriend, Seven easily could have slipped into the life that Khalil fell into. However, encouraged by Mav and Lisa, he stands up to Iesha, his mother, and seems to have a bright future ahead of him at college. Once again, the book portrays speaking out as the key to progress.

Chapters 22-26

Part 5: "Thirteen Weeks After It—The Decision"

Chapter 22 Summary

Seven weeks pass since Starr's testimony. The family moves into their new house in the nice neighborhood. April Ofrah calls to tell them that the grand jury will likely be make a decision soon, and Starr worries that she already knows what the decision will be.

At Chris's parents' house, he apologizes for White people, adding that he feels like he needs to say it. Starr says that they shouldn't be together and begins to list all the reasons they are so different. He counters all of them with reasons why they should be together. As a distraction, Starr tries to initiate sex, but Chris stops it because she is not in a good place. Starr cries instead, and they fall asleep.

Later, Seven calls, waking Starr up. He is worried because no one can find DeVante. Starr wakes Chris up and says that they will help look. Seven comes to pick them up and says Kenya told him DeVante is at King and Iesha's house. They drive over there and find DeVante beaten, lying in one of the bedrooms.

Kenya and her younger sister Lyric are also there, and Kenya tells them that King plans to kill DeVante when night falls. Seven wants to fight King when he hears that he shoved Kenya, but they hold him back. As they try to move

DeVante, Iesha enters. Although she believes DeVante got the beating he deserved, she tells Seven them all to take him and go. She tells him to take Kenya and Lyric, too. She goes back outside and distracts King by dancing to cover their exit.

Driving away, Seven is still mad at Iesha, but Starr points out that she did help. Plus, Iesha knows that King will be mad and that he will take it out on her. Still, she helped anyway.

On the radio, they hear that the grand jury decided not to indict Officer 115.

Chapter 23 Summary

On the drive home, they see the news spread through the neighborhood that the cop will not be charged with any crime in the killing of Khalil. Everyone in the car gets upset, and Chris is confused as to why Khalil won't get justice. The rest tell him that this is not uncommon.

Seven asks Starr what she wants to do. She says that she wants to do something, like protest or riot. She says she "did everything right, and it didn't make a fucking difference. I've gotten death threats, cops harassed my family, somebody shot into my house, all kinds of shit. And for what? Justice Khalil won't get?" (390). She tells Chris he doesn't have to agree, he just has to support her.

Kenya and Lyric stay with their grandmother while the rest of them drive over to Magnolia where the protestors were before. They park in front of Just Us for Justice. Half of the neighborhood is out in the streets. They rap along to Ice Cube and shout, "fuck the police" (393).

In the crowd, King Lords and Garden Disciples flip cars and someone throws a Molotov cocktail. The looting starts as people break into stores. When this happens, Starr and others in the crowd try to stop it. She doesn't want to be a part of that kind of riot.

Cops in riot gear appear, and the crowd continues to chant "fuck the police" (395). There is a small explosion and the crowd breaks up, as people run in different directions. Starr, Chris, DeVante, and Seven run back to Seven's car and drive away from the violence. They decide they should go to the store to help Mav in case looters try to break in. The run into police roadblocks and are forced to backtrack several times.

In the car, Seven and DeVante are impressed Chris knew the words to the NWA rap song. They also talk about the assumptions White people make and strange habits they have. Chris asks about "unusual" things that Black people name their kids, but the rest of them point out that unusual is just a point of view.

They hit more roadblocks, and Seven tells them that they'll have to go through Garden Disciple territory. This is where the worst of the riots happened last time and is also rival gang territory. Seven tells them they will be fine, but they can already hear gunshots nearby.

Chapter 24 Summary

It takes them a long time to find an unblocked road, and when they do, Seven's car runs out of gas and dies. Chris and Seven try pushing it toward a gas station but there is thick smoke in the air so they decide it will be faster to walk.

On the walk, as Chris asks Starr about the neighborhood, she realizes this is the first time he's been to Garden Heights. They come upon a crowd of protestors chanting "a hairbrush is not a gun" (407). They are on Carnation, which is where Khalil was killed.

April Ofrah leads the chant, shouting through a bullhorn. She gives it to someone else and comes over to Starr. She tells her that as her attorney, she has to tell her to get to safety. When Starr says she wants to speak, April has her fire her as her attorney. She then tells Starr that if anything goes wrong, she should run for cover behind a nearby bus. Starr understands, and April takes her over to stand on top of a patrol car and gives her the megaphone.

Starr speaks to the crowd, telling them that Officer 115 is a criminal who made deadly assumptions about her and Khalil. She tells the crowd "this isn't about how Khalil died. It's about the fact that he lived. His life mattered. Khalil lived!" (412). She shouts at the cops, who form a wall nearby. The crowd chants, and the police throw tear gas. Starr sees a can land nearby, so she jumps off the patrol car and throws the canister back toward the cops. Then "all hell breaks loose" (413).

She runs toward the bus and meets up with Chris, Seven, and DeVante, but they are engulfed in tear gas. It burns their eyes and they cannot see the bus anymore. Suddenly, a truck comes screeching up to them. In the back is Goon, one of the Cedar Grove King Lords who protected her before. They get into the truck and drive away. Also in the back is a reporter who asks her a few questions.

They drive to Mav's store and let themselves in with Seven's keys. Everyone in the truck rushes to pour milk over their faces to counteract the effects of the tear gas.

Goon takes extra milk and leaves to go help more people; the reporter asks to go with him.

The four kids are left in the store. Starr sees many missed calls and texts from Lisa and realizes they are in deep trouble. They decide to call home from the office so that the caller ID will prove where they are. However, before they can, a Molotov cocktail comes sailing in the window, setting everything on fire.

Chapter 25 Summary

The front exit is blocked by fire, so they try to reach the back door, but it is locked. Mav, Lisa and Carlos arrive just in time to unlock the door and let them all out. Coughing, Starr sees the neighborhood all coming to try to stop the flames, but they are too big to be doused. Nearby, King and some of his gang members lean on a car, watching. Mav calls him a coward for trying to burn children in the store. Carlos has to hold both him and Lisa back from running at King. Mr. Lewis shouts to the neighborhood that King burned down the store.

Police and a fire engine arrive, and while they put out the fire, Mr. Lewis tells the cops that King is responsible. Mav tells them too, snitching on King right in front of him. When the cops say they require an eyewitness who actually saw King do it, several people from the neighborhood claim they saw it. King and his gang members are arrested. The EMTs give the four kids oxygen to help with the smoke inhalation and tear gas. Starr holds Chris's hand while the sit on the curb.

They tell Mav and Lisa where they were all night. Mav comes over to talk to Chris. He respects him for being out in the hood so long and asks him to come to the boxing gym with him so he can learn more about the man dating his daughter.

Carlos comes over to tell DeVante that while he's glad he's ok, he's grounded. He tells everyone that they will be able to charge King for arson, but that means he'll be free by the end of the week. DeVante says he knows where King's stash is and decides to turn witness to help the neighborhood. Carlos promises to protect him from reprisals for becoming a snitch.

Chapter 26 Summary

The next morning, Starr gets up at 11. April Ofrah calls to apologize to Starr for putting her in danger but says that she is proud of her. She also tells Starr that she has a future in activism.

Starr gets a text from Hailey that says she is sorry about the decision and that she wants everything to be like it was. Starr texts back that it can never be like it was ever again and deletes Hailey's number.

The store is damaged, so they will have no income from it for a while, but the family will still make it work with the new house. They also vow not to abandon the community. They go to the store to meet with the insurance agent. Mr. Lewis is there and tells them that he decided to retire and leave Mav his shop so that he can expand the store. The insurance agent arrives to take stock of the damage and the family starts to clean up the burnt store.

Kenya stops by to say that King put Iesha in the hospital. She and Lyric will stay with their grandmother for a while. Still, she is relieved that King is in jail. She tells Starr she is sorry for calling Seven her brother only. She just always felt like Seven and Starr were ashamed of them. Starr admits this was once the truth because she "was ashamed of Garden Heights and everything in it. It seems stupid now though. I can't change where I come from or what I've been through, so why should I be ashamed of what makes me, me" (441). She tells Kenya she's not ashamed anymore and neither is Seven.

The book ends on a hopeful note. The family will rebuild the store. Starr decided that she will never stop fighting. She refuses to give up on a better ending to the story than what Khalil got. She promises "Khalil, I'll never forget. I'll never give up. I'll never be quiet" (444).

Chapters 22-26 Analysis

In the final section of the book, the tensions surrounding both the gang system in Garden Heights and the justice system come to a head. The grand jury finally comes to a decision and decides not to indict Officer 115 for Khalil's murder. Starr and the rest of the community are stunned and angry, and Starr allows this hate she receives to move her to action. She goes to join the riots and understands the feeling that moves people to organize and protest. She recognizes, however, the counterproductive and destructive results of the looting and violence that break out, in contrast to the mostly peaceful protests.

Starr's decision to join the demonstration plays into the book's idea of "doing everything right," a refrain that echoes similarly-themed Spike Lee film, *Do the Right Thing*. According to the tenets of "respectability politics," Black Americans are encouraged and expected to always behave in a responsible, legal manner as they wait for racial injustice to be rectified. Upon hearing the grand jury's decision, however, Starr comes to the realization that "doing everything right" won't fix social injustice. In *The New Jim Crow*, Michelle Alexander echoes this sentiment, writing, "The intuition underlying moral-uplift strategies is fundamentally sound: our communities will never thrive if we fail to respect ourselves and one another. As a liberation strategy, however, the politics of respectability are doomed to fail." (Alexander, Michelle. *The New Jim Crow*. New York: The New Press. 2010.)

At the protests, Starr again speaks out, bearing witness for Khalil. She also takes action, throwing a canister of tear gas back at the police. She once again uses the best weapon she has, which is her voice. The newspaper amplifies her voice, showing how activists can use the media to work on their behalf, rather than spread racist narratives.

In Garden Heights, Mav also uses his voice as a weapon, speaking out and naming King as the person behind the burning of his store, taking his cues from Mr. Lewis. The rest of the neighborhood also finds its voice and, crucially, DeVante agrees to speak out against King and his gang, virtually guaranteeing that King will be locked away for good. The power of speaking is once again shown to be the most effective means of change.

Meanwhile, Chris proves himself a true advocate of Starr and the Black community, staying by her side throughout the protest in Garden Heights and therefore becoming a witness himself. On the other hand, Hailey again refuses to acknowledge the problem of systemic racism in herself or in society. Starr finally cuts ties with her, realizing that the love she has for Hailey cannot overcome this impasse.

Finally, the book ends with Starr vowing never to stay silent, to keep speaking up for justice and fighting for change. This incredibly timely message is the point Thomas makes with the book itself.

CHARACTER ANALYSIS

Starr Carter

The main character and narrator of the book, Starr is the daughter of Mav and Lisa, and sister to Sekani and Seven. She is a junior in high school who struggles to reconcile her life at the predominantly White private school, Williamson Prep, with her upbringing and home life in Garden Heights, a predominantly Black and poor neighborhood with a prominent gang presence. Her life is hard in many respects; she saw her best friend shot and killed in a drive-by when they were 11 years old.

At the start of the story, she witnesses the murder of another friend, Khalil, by a police officer during a routine traffic stop. She struggles to find a way to advocate for Khalil without endangering herself or her family.

Starr also dates a White boy from Williamson, which presents certain problems for them both to overcome. However, throughout the novel, they grow closer as Starr opens up to Chris, who proves himself a firm advocate for her and her community.

At the end of the book, Starr uses her voice to speak out for Khalil and tell his side of the story, revealing the understood but rarely discussed systemic racism in the police force and in society at large.

Khalil Harris

Khalil is Starr's childhood friend and first crush. Although they grew apart since Starr started school at Williamson Prep, they reconnect at a party at the start of the novel. Khalil sells drugs, which Starr initially assumes is merely a decision he made as a Black boy growing up in Garden Heights. However, it is later revealed that Khalil more or less had no choice but to start working for King, because his mother owed the drug kingpin money. He also had very few other economic opportunities due to his upbringing.

Near the start of the novel, Khalil is shot and killed by Officer 115 during a traffic stop. Before being shot, the officer harassed Khalil, pulling him out of the car. Khalil as a character looms large over the rest of the novel as the community struggles to achieve justice for his death and as the media essentially puts him on trial for his own killing.

Maverick Carter

Maverick "Mav" Carter is Starr's father and a former member of the King Lords, one of two main gangs in Garden Heights. He took the fall for King, the leader of the gang, and served three years in prison when Starr was young, which is why he was allowed to leave the gang. He now owns a grocery store and is highly respected in the community.

Mav teaches his children the sayings of Malcolm X and the Black Panthers, telling them to always fight for what is right. However, he also gives them practical knowledge and skills for survival in Garden Heights. He is distrustful of Starr's White boyfriend Chris at first and also doesn't like his brother in law, Carlos, who is a cop. However, throughout the course of the novel he grows to respect them both.

In the end, he finally fully breaks free of King's control by snitching on him for trying to burn down the store with Starr inside. His actions inspire the rest of the community to do the same.

Lisa Carter

Lisa is Starr's mother and Mav's wife. She is a nurse who works at the neighborhood clinic who later gets a highly paying job at a hospital, allowing the family to move out of Garden Heights. She was wild as a girl, when she met Mav, and was put out of the house by her mother when she got pregnant with Starr as a teenager. However, being pregnant inspired her to clean up her act and be responsible for her children. She is a strict mother who nevertheless loves her children dearly and supports them in their beliefs. She is a frequent source of wisdom for Starr throughout the book.

Uncle Carlos

Carlos is Lisa's brother and Starr's uncle. He is a police officer who is married to a doctor. They live in a very nice gated community outside of Garden Heights. He helped raise Starr and her brothers when they were young, while Mav was in prison. As a result, Mav dislikes him.

Carlos is a source of safety for Starr throughout the novel, offering a unique perspective as a Black man and also a cop. Like Starr, he also exists in two worlds and struggles when they collide.

King

King is the leader of the King Lord gang and one of the antagonists of the book. He and Mav were friends when they were both in the gang, and King has a kind of respect for Mav, given that he took the fall for him on a drug charge. However, King is also a ruthless leader who sometimes terrorizes the Garden Heights community in order to maintain control.

When he finds out that Starr was the witness to the murder, King tries to intimidate her with increasingly violent acts. He attempts to burn her alive inside the store for dry snitching on him.

Chris Bryant

Chris is Starr's boyfriend from Williamson Prep. He comes from a very wealthy family but is sweet and shares many interests in common with Starr, such as a mutual love for *The Fresh Prince of Bel-Air* and sneakers. Throughout the novel, Chris is a well-meaning advocate for Starr and for the Black community in general. However, he confronts several assumptions and misconceptions he had about race and society as a result of his privileged upbringing. Starr gives him a new perspective, and he is receptive to new ways of thinking. He becomes a first-hand witness of the riots and proves himself a loyal and true ally for Starr and the community.

Seven

Seven is Starr's older half-brother and the son of Mav and Iesha. He is frequently caught between the Carter family and looking out for his Iesha and his sisters Kenya and Lyric from King's temper. He is smart and although he is accepted into college, he wants to turn down that opportunity to stay close to his family. Mav encourages him not to pass up the chance to do great things.

Seven is a protector in Starr's life, frequently coming to her defense and helping her make sense of her situation.

Hailey Grant

Hailey is one of Starr's best friends at Williamson Prep who plays on the basketball team with her. Starr and Hailey initially bonded because they in grief—Starr witnessed Natasha's death, and Hailey lost her mother to cancer. However, despite this bond, the friendship is unequal, with Hailey frequently ordering Starr and Maya around.

Hailey makes several casually racist comments to Starr but refuses to apologize or even acknowledge the harm of her words when confronted. She represents the insidious side of systemic racism in the novel, as she is a privileged White girl who cannot or will not see that racism is a problem at all. Eventually, Starr ends their friendship.

April Ofrah

April Ofrah is an attorney and one of the leaders of the Just Us for Justice organization. She is a source of information for the community who later acts as Starr's legal representation. She also leads the protests against Khalil's murder and the grand jury's decision not to indict his killer. During the riots, she encourages Starr to speak out.

April Ofrah represents the type of activist Starr might grow to be. She fights for her community and leads the charge against injustice.

DeVante

DeVante is a contemporary of Starr's and a member of the King Lords. At the beginning of the book, his brother is shot and killed at the party where Starr reconnects with Khalil. As a result of this tragedy, he wants to save the rest of his family from Garden Heights. To do this, he steals money from King, earning the wrath of the gang.

Knowing that Mav escaped the gang life, DeVante goes to him for help. Late in the book, he is found and beaten by the King Lords, but Starr, Seven and Chris help him escape. He goes through the events of the climax with the three of them. Ultimately, he decides to snitch on King in order to keep him in jail and help the neighborhood.

DeVante represents the life Khalil might have had, if he survived. He also helps Starr understand how easy and sometimes essential it is for young boys in the neighborhood to join a gang.

Officer 115, Brian Cruise

The police officer who shoots Khalil has a relatively small role in the story, but his presence looms large over the story. Starr refers to him as "115," which is his badge number. He racially profiles Khalil and Starr and pulls them over. When Khalil asks questions, he pulls him out of the car, harassing him. After Khalil attempts to ask Starr if she is alright, Officer 115 shoots him three times, killing him. He later says he believed that Khalil was reaching for a gun, but it is shown to be a hairbrush. He represents the common issue of systemic racism in the criminal justice system.

THEMES

Systemic Racism in the American Justice System and America at Large

The main theme of the book is the issue of systemic racism in America. Starr and her family experience racism in a variety of ways throughout the story. For example, Hailey makes a remark about fried chicken to Starr. Most overtly, of course, is the fact that Khalil is racially profiled by a police officer who shoots him on the assumption that he was going for a gun.

Despite the fact that Khalil was innocent and there was no reason for him to have been pulled over in the first place, the police and the White community immediately assume that he was in the wrong and Officer 115 was right. It takes ten weeks for a decision to even be made about whether the officer should be indicted, a frustratingly long time. Even then, the jury decides not to punish Officer 115 or even indicate in any way that his actions were wrong. This kind of decision is painfully true to life and highlights the deeply discriminatory justice systems in America. This kind of decision sends a message that Black lives matter less to the people in charge than White lives.

Less overtly, Starr struggles with the repercussions of systemic racism in her everyday life. She feels that she has to modulate her actions, her words, and her responses while she is at Williamson Prep to avoid being slapped with labels like "angry Black girl" and "ghetto." Known as code-switching, this is a survival tactic in navigating a school full of White people who do not even realize the threat of their preconceived notions. Even the fact that Garden Heights is described as a dangerous place full of gangs and drugs is subtly racist, as the implication is that Black communities are somehow inherently dangerous.

Chris is an example of a well-meaning White person who nevertheless does not realize how some of his assumptions and ideas are subtly racist. For example, Starr shows him how saying "I don't see race" is not helpful to disenfranchised communities. In fact, it is a privilege of the powerful segments of society to ignore racial issues.

More broadly, Mav and Starr discuss how communities like Garden Heights fall prey to drugs and gangs. Due to decades of redlining, targeted law enforcement, and other forms of institutionalized and personal racism, people growing up in poor Black communities often have fewer opportunities for stable employment and housing. Additionally, other segments of society, while maintaining barriers against these minority groups, also look down on them for their own lack of success. Eventually, when disenfranchised individuals grow "tired of choosing between lights and food," joining a gang or selling drugs seems like the only option (18).

Yet, as Mav points out, the drugs come from outside, from rich people who only get richer. The struggling minority communities thus continue to struggle while the privileged community benefits, and the cycle of systemic racism continues.

The Strength of Community Efforts to Fight Injustice

Community is an important theme throughout the book. Although Garden Heights is economically disadvantaged and has issues with gangs, it is ultimately a community that pulls together to protect and support one another. As Starr describes it: "people around here don't have much, but they help each other out as best they can. It's this strange, dysfunctional-as-hell family, but it's still a family" (328-9).

When Khalil is murdered, the entire community mobilizes to protest. Similarly, when Mav and Mr. Lewis snitch on King, the rest of the neighborhood steps up to support them. Even in little ways, like when people in the neighborhood greet Starr as they pass, Garden Heights is shown to be a true community.

For Starr, the question of community has extra depth, however. She is caught between two worlds and spends much of the book struggling to reconcile these two sides of her life. In the end, she realizes that she can build a community that is uniquely her own by including people from Williamson and people from Garden Heights.

Police Brutality and Racial Profiling

The problem of police brutality is a theme that looms over the entire story. Khalil's murder by a police officer during a traffic stops is symbolic of the many deadly and damaging acts of police violence that are committed against Black individuals and other minorities on a shockingly frequent basis. The way the justice system handles this act of violence—slowly and ultimately with no repercussions—is just one example of how police brutality is brushed under the carpet and, horrifically, seen as almost a normal occurrence.

Starr and her family suspect early on that there will be no true justice for Khalil; they and the community of Garden Heights have seen this all before. Other encounters with the police bear a similar threat of violence, such as when the two cops stop to intervene in Mav and Mr. Lewis's argument. The police force Mav to the ground and search him, even though he did nothing to indicate he was a threat. In short, the police intervention exacerbates a situation that was already under control. Events like this go a long way in explaining why distrust of the police is so high in communities where officers take an overly proactive role in policing.

When the protests start, the police treat the protestors as criminals. Starr witnesses firsthand how the cops throw tear gas into a crowd doing nothing more threatening than chanting. In response to the riots and looting, the police send in armored tanks and other heavy equipment, as if they are going to war against a community merely trying to express its dissatisfaction with the injustice committed against one of their own.

Tupac Shakur's THUG LIFE

Tupac Shakur's THUG LIFE saying—which became the basis for his hip hop group name and his famous stomach tattoo—is a major recurring symbol in the book and the source of the novel's title as well. THUG LIFE is an acronym that stands for "The Hate U Give Little Infants Fucks Everybody" (17). At key points in the novel, Starr discusses the meaning behind THUG LIFE, first with Khalil and then with Mav. In her room in their new house, she prominently displays a poster of Tupac.

The idea behind Tupac's THUG LIFE is the cyclical nature of hatred and the damage done by systems in which hatred is ingrained. Social systems are designed to preference some groups over others, often along racial lines. As a result, the privileged groups hate and fear the disenfranchised groups.

This plays out clearly in the book. The ingrained hatred that leads Officer 115 to shoot Khalil exacerbates the hatred and mistrust that the Garden Heights community feels for the police. This leads to the protests and riots, which the police, informed by hatred, respond to with violence. This violence begets more violence, and the cycle continues.

Starr attempts to break this cycle by speaking out, telling the side of the story that is not often told. Telling this story encourages both sides to examine their preconceptions and biases. In turn, this leads to understanding, which is the only way to fight back against the cycle of hate.

The Hairbrush

The hairbrush that Khalil had in his car at the time of his murder is transformed into a symbol of protest by the Just Us for Justice activists and the Garden Heights community in general. After the shooting, Officer 115 claims that he thought he saw Khalil reach for a gun in his car door. The truth is that what he claims looked like a gun was the hairbrush that Khalil used to brush his fade. Although Officer 115's explanation is more or less accepted as rational by the media, the White community, and, seemingly, by the grand jury, it is seen as absurd by the Black community.

For this reason, April Ofrah and the rest of the protestors at the end of the book all hold hairbrushes. They chant "a hairbrush is not a gun" over and over (407). They use the hairbrush to symbolize the injustice of Khalil's death. Officer 115 saw the brush handle in the door, but it was only because Khalil was Black that he assumed it was a gun and not anything else. By pointing out the fact that a police officer immediately assumed the object was a gun, the protesters show that racist ideas and assumptions are incredibly ingrained in law enforcement and American society in general.

Sneakers

Sneakers are a recurring symbol in the book, largely due to the fact that Starr is a self-proclaimed sneaker head. Her shoes are important to her, and she goes out of her way to find limited-edition and otherwise special shoes. She also keeps them in pristine condition and even cleans pairs for other people.

For Starr, her sneakers are one of the main ways she expresses her individuality. At Williamson Prep, she has to wear a uniform, but "I can make sure my sneakers are always dope and my backpack matches them" (71). There is much in her life that she cannot control, so she takes extra care in her choice of footwear.

She also notices other people's sneakers, especially people to whom she feels a connection. When she reconnects with Khalil at the start of the book, she notes his Jordans, of which she has a similar pair. She also points out that she and Chris frequently match footwear, showing that their connection is deep.

IMPORTANT QUOTES

1. "Funny how it works with white kids though. It's dope to be black until it's hard to be black." (Chapter 1, Page 11)

   Starr struggles throughout the book to walk between two worlds: the predominantly Black world of Garden Heights and the predominantly White world of Williamson. At Williamson, she walks a fine line between being seen as cool and interesting just because of her skin color and being looked down on for exactly the same reason. In response to this conflicted identity, Starr learns to code-switch as a strategy for navigating her dual worlds.

2. "The Hate U Give Little Infants Fucks Everybody." (Chapter 1, Page 17)

   In the very first chapter, Khalil explains what Tupac's THUG LIFE ideology stands for. This is the source of the book's title and a major theme throughout the work. This line is especially tragic as, in the next chapter, Khalil dies as a result of the systemic and cyclical violence that Tupac's words defined. The hate that causes his death results in more violence and hate, leading to the riots that potentially have serious fallout for Starr and her community.

3. "I've seen it happen over and over again: a black person gets killed just for being black, and all hell breaks loose. I've Tweeted RIP hashtags, reblogged pictures on Tumblr, and signed every petition out there. I always said that if I saw it happen to somebody, I would have the loudest voice, making sure the world knew what

went down. Now I am that person, and I'm too afraid to speak." (Chapter 3, Page 35)

Starr explains how Khalil's death and the lack of justice that follows is, tragically, not an anomalous event in Garden Heights nor in America in general. This quote speaks to the way that police brutality and the deaths of innocent Black people in America are typically handled: it is news for a time, people share the story on social media, there is outrage, and sometimes protests. However, there is rarely significant justice for the victim. In this section, Starr sees how easy it is to say that she would speak out against injustice when it is hypothetical, but how frightening it is to do so when it directly affects her life.

4. "Don't let them put words in your mouth. God gave you a brain. You don't need theirs." (Chapter 4, Page 58)

Mav tells Starr not to let the police officers twist her words when she goes to tell them her side of the story. Mav and Starr know that, when a police shooting happens—especially one involving a Black man—the media and authorities always blame the victim, explicitly or by implication. This turns out to be wise advice, as the police officers frame the interview almost entirely around Khalil and his actions, rather than Officer 115's.

5. "Williamson Starr doesn't use slang—if a rapper would say it, she doesn't say it, even if her white friends do. Slang makes them cool. Slang makes her 'hood.' Williamson Starr holds her tongue when people piss her off so nobody will think she's the 'angry black girl.' Williamson Starr is approachable. No stank-eyes, none

of that. Williamson Starr is no confrontational. Basically, Williamson Starr doesn't give anyone a reason to call her ghetto. I can't stand myself for doing it, but I do it anyway." (Chapter 5, Page 71)

This passage again shows the fine line Starr must walk while attending the predominantly White and wealthy school, Williamson Prep. She cannot be who she truly is or display strong emotions for fear of playing into people's preconceived notions and stereotypes. She knows that being labeled "ghetto" or "hood" would make her life difficult and might mean she would not have friends, and so she takes care to maintain a façade at school.

6. "I hope none of them ask about my spring break. They went to Taipei, the Bahamas, Harry Potter World. I stayed in the hood and saw a cop kill my friend." (Chapter 5, Page 77)

    This quote highlights the differences that Starr feels at Williamson every day, but which her white friends and classmates likely never even imagine. Being raised in privileged households, they talk about expensive vacations and other luxuries, never considering that they are among a very small section of American society who can afford these things. Starr must keep quiet and hope no one notices that she does not share these experiences with them for fear of being labeled an outsider.

7. "Khalil's eyes stare back at me, and I realize my mom's right. Ms. Brenda is Khalil's momma. Regardless." (Chapter 5, Page 92)

Starr believes that Khalil's mother, Brenda, was a poor mother to him, as she was the reason he got into drug dealing and, therefore, may have indirectly contributed to his death. However, she comes to understand that the pain Brenda feels at his death is no less real. She was still his mother; she still loved him. She realizes it is not her place to judge Brenda, either.

8. "You can say something racist and not be a racist!" (Chapter 7, Page 112)

   This quote comes after a crucial moment in the book, when Hailey casually makes a racist comment to Starr about fried chicken. Hailey reacts defensively, but Starr tries to explain that her intention is not to call Hailey a racist but to point out that the comment was racist. She attempts to draw attention to the unconscious racial biases that Hailey internalizes. However, Hailey refuses to think critically about her words or why she said them, believing that the comment was harmless and that Starr simply overreacted.

9. "Sometimes you can do everything right and things will still go wrong. The key is to never stop doing right." (Chapter 9, Page 154)

   Lisa shares this wisdom with Starr after she talks to the police—trying to do the right thing—but nothing seems to come of it. This is a major message in the book: that things don't always work out in a fair way and justice is not always served, but that this is no reason not to keep striving for a better future. In fact, that is the only way to make the future better than the present. It also highlights the extent to which entreaties rooted in respectability politics to "do everything right" often fail as strategies for achieving racial justice.

10. "Her words used to have power. If she said it was fine, it was fine. But after you've held two people as they took their last breaths, words like that don't mean shit anymore." (Chapter 10, Page 165)

In this passage, Starr expresses how her perspective changed since the death of Khalil. She witnessed firsthand how frightening, unjust, and deadly the world can be, especially for members of the Black community. Therefore, she is no longer comforted when her mother tells her that everything in fine. She knows that everything is not fine.

11. "'Exactly. Drugs come from somewhere, and they're destroying our community,' he says. 'You got folks like Brenda, who think they need them to survive, and then you got the Khalils, who think they need to sell them to survive. The Brendas can't get jobs unless they're clean, and they can't pay for rehab unless they got jobs. When the Khalils get arrested for selling drugs, they either spend most of their life in prison, another billion-dollar industry, or they have a hard time getting a real job and probably start selling drugs again. That's the hate they're giving us, baby, a system designed against us. That's Thug Life.'" (Chapter 10, Page 170)

In this passage, Mav and Starr discuss Tupac's THUG LIFE ideology as it applies to communities like Garden Heights. The neighborhood is seen as violent, full of drugs and gangs, and ultimately a dangerous place. By extension, the people who live there are looked down on by the wealthier, predominantly White segments of society that hold the most political and economic power. However, the same systems that are designed to help the privileged classes achieve success and wealth keep individuals in disadvantaged communities from making the same advances. Instead, people like Khalil are caught in a self-perpetuating cycle that leads to the drug trade and gangs.

12. "They're so damn excited about getting a day off. Khalil's in a grave. He can't get a day off from that shit. I live it every single day too." (Chapter 11, Page 183)

    This quote is in response to Starr learning that the students of Williamson plan to stage a protest for Khalil just to get out of class. Starr is sickened and infuriated that his unjust killing is used as nothing more than an excuse to cut class. The students of Williamson don't truly care about Khalil and cannot even imagine what it would be like to be Starr in this situation.

13. "They act like I'm the official representative of the black race and they owe me an explanation. I think I understand though. If I sit out a protest, I'm making a statement, but if they sit out a protest, they look racist." (Chapter 11, Page 186)

    Some White students also refuse to participate in the fake protest, and Starr finds them coming up to her to explain why. On the one hand, Starr does not like to be singled out by her skin color and used as a way for people to express White guilt. However, she also understands that the students mean well, because they do not want her to assume they refused to protest for racist reasons.

14. "The only way people will know his side of the story is if I speak out." (Chapter 12, Page 218)

    In this section, Starr finally resolves to speak out and tell her side of the story. She sees White voices and the voices of the establishment control the narrative. If she doesn't bear witness as the only person who saw the shooting happen, then no one will defend Khalil, and he will be blamed for his own death.

15. "That's the problem. We let people say stuff, and they say it so much that it becomes okay to them and normal for us. What's the point of having a voice if you're gonna be silent in those moments you shouldn't be?" (Chapter 14, Page 252)

    When Maya and Starr realize that Hailey routinely says casually racist things to both of them, they decide to form what they call a "minority alliance" and agree not to let her say those things unchallenged anymore. Letting subtle racism go unaddressed is one of the ways that major, systemic racism is allowed to flourish. This is another example of Starr realizing that using her voice, is her best weapon against hate of all kinds.

16. "'He was more than any bad decision he made,' he says. 'I hate that I let myself fall into that mind-set of trying to rationalize his death. And at the end of the day, you don't kill someone for opening a car door. If you do, you shouldn't be a cop.'" (Chapter 14, Page 256)

    In this passage, Carlos realizes that he himself internalized a systemically racist mindset as a result of his affiliation as a police officer. Like many others, he immediately jumped to conclusions about Khalil when he heard about the murder, looking for things like Khalil's history as a drug dealer as an explanation for why Officer 115 shot him. However, Carlos realizes that this is just internalized hatred and that there is no excuse for shooting someone for opening a car door.

17. "Well, Munch, you have to decide if the relationship is worth salvaging. Make a list of the good stuff, then make a list of the bad stuff. If one outweighs the other, then you know what you gotta do. Trust me, that method hasn't failed me yet." (Chapter 15, Page 264)

When Starr tells her mother about Hailey's racist comments, Lisa advises her to take stock of the relationship and decide if her friendship with Hailey is worth fighting for. She doesn't tell Starr to abandon her completely, but also doesn't advise her to put up with Hailey's behavior just to save the friendship. Ultimately, Hailey's refusal to fully acknowledge her internalized racist biases causes Starr to extricate herself from a toxic friendship.

18. "At an early age I learned that people make mistakes, and you have to decide if their mistakes are bigger than your love for them." (Chapter 15, Page 264)

Lisa tells Starr that growing up with an alcoholic mother in less than ideal circumstances taught her that no one is perfect. Life is about forgiveness and understanding, not leaving people you love behind when they make mistakes. However, Lisa does not tell Starr that understanding is always required. Instead, she encourages her to weigh her love and connection for a person against the seriousness of their mistakes and make a decision that way.

19. "'Right. This all happened because he'—I can't say his name—'assumed that we were up to no good. Because we're black and because of where we live. We were just two kids, minding our business, you know? His assumption killed Khalil. It could've killed me.'" (Chapter 16, Page 290)

*In giving her interview to the local news station, Starr
tries to put into words the issue of systemic racism: it is
that the baseline assumption by people in power is that
Black people are somehow dangerous or deceptive.
This is true not just of individuals but of systems like the
criminal justice system. The individuals in power are
most often White and the systems were generally
created by majority-White individuals as well to
maintain a social stratification built to a large extent
around race.*

20. "People around here don't have much, but they help
each other out as best they can. It's this strange,
dysfunctional-as-hell family, but it's still a family."
(Chapter 19, Pages 328-29)

*In this quote, Starr sees how her community of Garden
Heights—of which she was previously ashamed—is a
family. The people who live there may not have the
most money or economic power, but they care about
one another and will work to protect one another. This
is seen again later when the neighborhood comes
together to support Mav when he snitches on King.*

21. "'Brave doesn't mean you're not scared, Starr,' she
says. 'It means you go on even though you're scared.
And you're doing that.'" (Chapter 19, Page 331)

*Again, Lisa acts as a voice of wisdom for Starr in this
section. She explains that bravery is not a lack of fear,
but instead it is the courage to do what is right and
speak out even in the face of fear. This lesson helps
Starr through her grand jury testimony and again later
when she speaks to the crowd at the protests. It
becomes a kind of mantra for her at the end of the book
as she vows never to be silent.*

22. "They with a capital T. There's Them and then there's Us. Sometimes They look like Us and don't realize They are Us." (Chapter 20, Page 343)

After Starr gets into a fight at school, Lisa makes a remark about her behaving just like They would expect. Essentially, she broke her own rules and played into the stereotypes at school that she usually tries to avoid. However, Starr realizes that there always exists a dichotomy of Them and Us. The powerful, majority-White community sees the disenfranchised majority-Black community as "Them," but the reverse is also true. This mindset is adversarial and is the result of unconscious biases born from unchallenged systemic racism.

23. "I never know which Starr I should be. I can use some slang, but not too much slang, some attitude, but not too much attitude, so I'm not a 'sassy black girl.' I have to watch what I say and how I say it, but I can't sound 'white.'" (Chapter 21, Page 357)

Again, Starr articulates the fine line she walks in her day-to-day life. While at school, she tries not to act "too Black," but in her home community, she has to try not to act "too white." Since she goes to a private, majority-White school, there is a danger that the Black community will stereotype her in the same way that her White classmates might stereotype her.

24. "People say misery loves company, but I think it's like that with anger too." (Chapter 23, Page 393)

Witnessing the protests and how they turn quickly into riots, Starr realizes that anger is a unifying factor for a community. However, while the power of collective anger can be constructive, such as how the protestors unite around a message against injustice, she also sees that it can easily become destructive when not channeled toward a goal.

25. "This isn't about how Khalil died. It's about the fact that he lived. His life mattered. Khalil lived!" (Chapter 24, Page 412)

At the protests, Starr speaks to the group organized by Just Us for Justice. She puts into words the thing that matters to her most: bearing witness to Khalil's life. Yes, they are protesting the injustice of his death, but Khalil was more than just the way he died. It is Starr's mission to make sure his life is not forgotten.

ESSAY TOPICS

1. Tupac's THUG LIFE explanation is a major theme of the book. How do you see THUG LIFE playing out in the real world today, possibly even in your community? Can you relate any recent events to the idea of THUG LIFE?

2. THUG LIFE refers to the self-perpetuating cycle of hatred but does not necessarily offer a solution. How does author Angie Thomas address this? Does she offer a solution or is the answer more complicated? How do you think you can fight against this cycle?

3. How does this book provide a voice and a perspective that is often overlooked?

4. Starr spends much of the book trying to decide "which Starr" to be in any given situation. How is this resolved at the end of the novel? Have you ever felt like you need to edit yourself to fit in?

5. How does social media factor into the story and affect Starr's life? What do you think this says about the power of social media? Do you see its power in your own life?

6. How does Starr's relationship with Chris change and grow throughout the novel? What do they learn about each other? What preconceptions did they each have that were challenged?

7. Starr tells Hailey, "You can say something racist and not be racist." What does this mean? Do you agree? How would you handle it if you heard someone say

something racist in the way that Hailey did? Have you ever been in a situation like this? If so, what happened?

8. How does Starr's opinion of the police change throughout the novel? What does Carlos struggle with as a police officer himself?

9. How is Maya's story similar to Starr's? How is it different? If the novel was written from her perspective, how would it change, do you think?

10. There is a lot of discussion about how Khalil ended up as a drug dealer and how many of the young men in the community do the same. Do you think something like this happened to King? How do you think he ended up as the character that he is? How does THUG LIFE apply to him?

Made in the USA
Middletown, DE
22 July 2022